Tell 'em About It!

Tell 'em About It!

Jerry Gold

Writers Club Press
San Jose New York Lincoln Shanghai

Tell 'em About It!

Writers Club Press
an imprint of iUniverse.com, Inc.

For information address:
iUniverse.com, Inc.
5220 S 16th, Ste. 200
Lincoln, NE 68512
www.iuniverse.com

ISBN: 0-595-18275-5

Printed in the United States of America

This book is dedicated to all those who became public speakers by attending my classes. Readers of this book will join the long list!

If someone were to ask you, What is the greatest fear people have, how would you respond? Fear of dying? Nah, fear of death (surprise!) only ties for 6th place on the long list with sickness. (makes sense to me!) How about fearing the dark? Not by a long shot. 12th place is as high as the dark rates. OK, one more guess. Fear of heights? Close, 2nd on the list. Here it is. Of all people polled, 41% said the greatest fear in life is SPEAKING IN FRONT OF A GROUP OF PEOPLE! *(Book of Answers, Prentice Hall Press, 1990)* Does this mean that people would rather die than speak in front of an audience? Of course not. The good news is you can improve on your efforts to eliminate that fear right now!

Note that this book does not come equipped with a gun, so you can not be forced by someone to make you stand up and talk. However, based on the many seminars I have given, and the results I have seen, I KNOW YOU CAN DO IT! I will point out in this book aids to make it easy for you to get up there and be a competent speaker. Along the way I will give you some tips that will make the audience sit on the edge of their seats and listen to you as though you were telling the secrets of life, because, actually, when you are up on that stage, you will be so motivated, so sure of your subject, so confident in yourself, you will give the impression you ARE telling the secrets of life.

Now it is time for the PROMISE. When you make the decision to become a public speaker you must promise yourself that you will stand up and PRACTICE! PRACTICE! PRACTICE! In fact, you should practice every chance you get.

Let's face it. There is only one person in this world that will make you a great public speaker. Guess who? You. You must actually make the effort to DO the things you want to do, because the more you DO them, obviously, the easier they will become to DO. You are now starting on the road to gaining new abilities and knowledge which will greatly enhance your skills in getting your point across to those to which you communicate, both through public speeches and personal discussions. Trust me. Now stand up. If there is anyone else in the room, face them, if not, look into the nearest mirror and say this-I PROMISE TO PRACTICE SPEAKING, EITHER IN FRONT OF OTHERS, OR A MIRROR, EVERY CHANCE I GET! Did anyone look at you funny? Of course not. Why? Because they know you are trying to better yourself. And you will! You are going to use proper English and diction.

You are going to speak logically, putting ideas in their proper order and not ramble on and on. You are going to gain knowledge while preparing for your speeches. You will speak directly to the point, make the point, and move on to the next item of business. You will speak with emotion and SHOW that emotion so your listening audience will know you are sincere. You WILL be motivated because you will know what you are talking about and will be prepared to talk about it. You will be more confident in yourself than ever before, because you will be in control of yourself and the speaking engagement; you will be the expert. This new found confidence will increase as you progress, making it easier to accomplish any task set before you. Now, let's get to it. It is time to start making you a better person. I will start off this way:

So it's 1958. I am seated in the cavernous auditorium of South Philadelphia High School. Yes, the famous school of the stars. Some of the people who were attending SPHS at the time were Frankie Avalon, Bobby Rydell, and Ernest Evans, also known as Chubby Checker. Down through the years these people also passed through these hallowed halls: Marion Anderson, Eddie Fisher, Jack Klugman, Angelo Dundee, Mario Lanza and others. One may have thought that all you had to do was just go to the school and you would be famous. Well, of course it did not work out that way. Look at me! Anyway, here I am, sitting in the hall with over 500 other students, the graduating class of 1958. You see, we were each to have memorized a preselected article out of old school yearbooks and present that passage to the class as a speech.

This was an audition for valedictorian at the class's graduation ceremony. As we were called by the teacher, one by one, we would leave our seat, sidle over to the nearest aisle, make our way to the stage steps, climb the steps up to the stage, and recite to the entire class. I am sure most of the kids were nervous. I was not. Not only could I not wait to get up and speak, I could not wait to sit back down. I was sitting next to the lovely Elaine, the object of my teenage dreams. Was she going to be impressed with me? You had better believe it. I ignored the current proceedings and was about to ask her about Saturday night when from out of the speakers set in the ceiling came the voice.

"Jerry Gold, it's your turn!" I got up and made my way to the podium; it was a long trip, and my footsteps echoed throughout the 1200 seat room. I set myself firmly at the lectern, looked first to the right of the audience, then the left. I spoke out in my strongest voice-"Franklin D. Roosevelt was a great president!............." Then it happened. My mind was a blank! Well, what did I expect? I had not prepared. I had never studied the piece. I thought I would have been able to remember it! I never had considered this situation happening. I stared out into all the space in front of me, my class forgotten, never mind my date with Elaine. Moisture started running down the sides of my head. I could feel my face turning red. I thought the entire class was laughing at me, the fabulous Elaine leading them. I had forgotten the rest of my speech! I stood there for an eternity until, mercifully, the voice rained down from the roof. "You may sit down now, Mr. Gold!" Returning to my seat took longer than anything I ever did in my life.

I sat down, avoiding Elaine as much as I could, too embarrassed to say anything. The next speaker was on her way to the stage. Elaine leaned over to me and whispered in my ear: "I gave you an `A'," she said, to my great surprise. "How could you do that? I only said one sentence!" "I know, she replied, BUT YOU SAID IT SO WELL!"

Needless to say, I was not the class valedictorian, but what a valuable lesson I had learned. Just think how I might have fared if I had only studied the speech as I should have! Certainly all of us in the class had plenty of time to complete this assignment. We were to have picked our subjects over a month in advance. But, I blew it. One can never second guess about the future, but then again.....

I joined the United States Marine Corps after high school, and when I finished my tour four years later, I decided to go back to school. I attended business college and one of those courses was public speaking. Each class member was to deliver a series of speeches throughout the term, the first one being a demonstrative talk. You had to show how something worked.

Since I was a waiter at banquets at the time, I often showed up in class wearing a tuxedo, so the subject of my first speech was "Tying a bow tie". It was a very good talk, except for one thing. During the course of the talk I found that my hands were not doing what I was saying they should be doing! The knot was not right. Suddenly, I had an inspiration. I grabbed one end of the tie and pulled straight up, simulating a noose, while hanging my tongue out of the side of my mouth. "This isn't so difficult, I said, once you get the hang of it!" The class laughed, and so did the teacher. While they laughed, I untied the tie and calmly started over. The knot was tied by the time I finished the talk. Success! An A+! The rest of the term was a breeze.

So there were two speeches early in my life that were instrumental in revealing that I had a talent. But did I take advantage of it? Nah. I just went through life trying to succeed as best I could. It was not until later that I finally realized my potential. But hey, this is not helping you any. Or is it? Obviously I did not practice for either of those speeches the way I should have, although I did know how to tie that bow tie. I knew how to do it so well that even when I made a mistake I was able to turn the error into a plus. So what do I want to say here? IF YOU LEARN NOTHING ELSE IN THIS BOOK, (I can't imagine that!) LEARN THIS: KNOW YOUR SUBJECT! KNOW YOUR SUBJECT!! KNOW YOUR SUBJECT!!! Forceful enough for ya? Here is another story to drive the point home. By the way, all these stories I relate throughout these pages are true. Remember that statement, I will talk about it later!

During the late 1970's I became the founder and president of a group of high school parents which numbered over 11,000 people. During the six month period it took to organize the group, I had spoken at virtually every high school in Philadelphia and, at one point, found myself back on the very stage at South Philly High where I had performed so miserably almost 25 years earlier. I was leading a rally that evening against busing and more than 1000 folks had shown up in support. My job that evening, after the welcoming speech, was to introduce the half dozen or so councilmen sitting with me. These were the guys who wrote the laws for our city. Each of them answered directly to the mayor. (You know you need some big guns at a rally!) I had just called the next to last speaker and had returned to my seat when I noticed a man rushing down the side of the room towards the stage. He mounted the steps and sat down next to me. I recognized him as a councilman. While adjusting his tie, he apologized for being late because of a previous appointment. Leaning past me he spoke to the legislator sitting next to me on the other side. "Hey Jim, what are we talking about here?" "Busing", said Jim. "Are we for or against?" "Against," answered Jim. "Got it!" Soon after, our late arriving friend stood up and gave one of the most forceful and engaging speeches of the evening. In fact, it made the newspapers the following day. He advocated driving buses off a pier, relating that venture to the dumping of tea into the Boston harbor. Did he make his point? You had better believe it! In any case, the question arises-what do you think the outcome would have been, had Jim said we were FOR busing? Do you think the speech would have been as good? Undoubtably. If you know your subject, backwards and forwards, there's no room for error. You can not go wrong! You are the expert! You are so sure of yourself there's no chance for failure! You can even change the point of the story to suit the crowd! To believe in what you are stating is only accomplished by the fact of KNOWING what you are stating! You know how to get to Carnegie Hall don't you? PRACTICE! PRACTICE!! PRACTICE!!!

So what will you talk about? Of course that will depend a lot on who you are speaking to and why. You may be called on to merely introduce another speaker (the term 'merely' pertains to the length of the speech, not its importance), to present a report, or best of all, to be the featured speaker at an event. But remember, whatever you talk about, YOU are the expert! YOU are the person they came to hear. You are confident, you are motivated; get up and talk to them! Whatever the talk may be, you will, of course, want to make the greatest impression possible. How can you make a great impression, you ask? Simple. Know what it is you are talking about and why. Know it backwards and forward and realize that everyone will be greatly impressed. Then realize that you CAN do this! AND YOU CAN! AND WILL! The first thing you will need to do is to realize your own personal abilities and strengths. We all have them, along with weaknesses and fears (there's that word again!). But this is the difference between us, the people who will dedicate time and effort to better ourselves, and those who will not. We appreciate and take advantage of our strengths and personal abilities to better our lives and attempt to decrease or eliminate the weaknesses which hold us back. You realize that there is only one way to learn how to accomplish anything, and that is to Do IT! Soooooo.... You need to sit down and list these debits and credits of yours. Note your strong points and be aware of them so you can take advantage of them whenever needed.

Can you make people laugh? Do so! Is it easy for you to retain numbers or facts and figures in your head and to call them up quickly? Do so! Can you vary the pitch, tone or tempo of your voice easily? Take advantage of this skill! You are one step ahead already. Perhaps you're not really sure about those abilities that will allow you to excel. Take your time when you create your list and, of course, be honest with yourself. No one has to see it so tell it like it is. As you progress, (and you will, because you will devote yourself to to the accomplishment of it), you will find that your list of abilities and strengths will grow, while on the other side of the ledger, the list of your weaknesses will shrink.

Now put this book down, get pen and paper or turn on your computer, and concentrate on putting down on paper just how it is you feel about yourself. Remember, be honest! The deeper you get into yourself the more you can change for the better. Now, go do it!

Back so soon? Now that you have taken the time and trouble to find out about yourself, what do you intend doing about it? OK, sit back and digest this next little piece, a story I have told on more than one occasion, to many diverse groups!

In 1990, I won a contest. The prize was a week for two in Maui. That's in Hawaii, You know. To my Hawaiian friends-Maui no ka oi! (Maui is number 1!) My wife and I went and we had the time of our lives, however it came back to haunt us a few years later. A short time after returning home, a form was sent to me by the company who awarded us the trip. This form, a 1099, showed the worth of the vacation for purposes of paying income taxes was approximately $6,000.00. I was not too thrilled upon getting this bit of information, because I knew that companies do not usually pay retail in these situations. Three weeks later, however, a new form was sent to me stating the revised value-$3500.00! When it was time to file I sent all the required papers to the IRS. So ended the 1990 tax year. Until 1993. I received a letter from the IRS in February, 1993. We propose, it read, to raise your taxes $1300.00 for the year 1990. Please respond or contact us if you disagree. (Of course I am only giving you the highlights of the letter; a long list of what would happen to me if I disagreed was included!) I immediately called the company who awarded me the trip and read the letter to their man in finance. Could he help me? He sent me an explanation and another set of 1099s which I forwarded to the IRS and then waited. And waited. Another three weeks went by. Another letter from IRS. "Your file cannot as yet be closed. We have not received enough corroborative information." What was going on here! I called the regional office of the IRS in Atlanta. A lovely lady, Ms. G., told me she would investigate and call me back. Amazingly, she did, one hour later. I was told that all the IRS had received three weeks ago was a handwritten note from me explaining the error, which was that someone, either trying to increase revenues or just being dumb, had added together two items that were not supposed to be added! One form was a corrected copy of the other! Ms. G. asked me if I would be so kind as to fax her another set of copies. I agreed, but had to wait until the following morning to do so. Twenty minutes after I sent the fax I called Atlanta again, and asked to speak to Ms. G. I was told she was off that day! That day happened to be the Friday preceding the

Memorial Day weekend, so I had to wait until the following Tuesday to find out the verdict. Ms. G. called me, and, in fact, told me she would close the account. Everything was A-OK. The harrowing experience was over. I never heard from IRS again. Consider this last entry as a speech. How would you deliver it? There is obviously more than one view here. I could focus on the fact that mistakes were made, perhaps by new employees, and praise Ms. G. and all her good work. I could also call the IRS an agency full of stupid people, incompetent in the undertaking of their jobs, and generally, chastise everyone involved. Or, I could speak humorously about the situation, just like a talk show guest. By the way, you do not want to hold up a copy of your 1099 or photos of your trip, because the folks sitting in the back row will not be able to see them. (More about audio/visual aids later!) Remember I said something about true to life stories? Without a doubt there is no better way to relate to an audience than to tell them something that is real, that they can understand, that they realize can happen to them.

There is, though, something else to consider. What if you are sitting in the audience, and you hear this talk, condemning the IRS, and you happen to be an employee of that agency? How happy will you be? Got it? Not only do you need to be knowledgeable in your subject, you need to ensure that your talk will be appropriate to your audience. Now if you do not mind offending the group, and do not wish to be invited back for another speech, do not worry about the makeup of the audience. But you are bright enough to know that a speaker must make an assessment of the group to whom he/she will be speaking. Is this an adult audience? Are they familiar with the subject, at least enough so that you will not be talking over their heads? If adult, are they working people, generally, or is this a retired group? You MUST determine what the audience wants to hear, and create your speech to meet that need. When called upon to speak at an engagement, it is sometimes important for you to answer questions which will enable you to be accepted as an expert. In addition, there are basic questions that you as a speaker must ask of your host. How many people will be in attendance? What size is the room and how will the seating be laid out? Is there an audio system and will you need it? Will food be served and will you speak during the eating period? Should you accept questions from the audience? FIND OUT ABOUT THE AUDIENCE!!! More on these questions later. In a pinch, once you become adept at all this, (it won't take long, I promise!) you can improvise. The following is an example of what I mean.

Some time ago, I was asked to give a series of book reviews for a ladies' group. I had done many of these before; basically, I am always reading three to five books at a time anyway, why not capitalize on it? I normally devote ten minutes to each book. I note some of the action, not giving away anything, trying to make the plot seem interesting enough that some (at least) of the audience would want to read it. So here I am, driving to the ladies club meeting place, books stacked up next to me in the passenger seat. I glance at the book on top and realize it is a Stephen King book! Oh oh. I started to panic. Yeah, you heard right. I admit it. Anybody who says he is never nervous is either lying or dead. Here I am going to speak to a group of which the median age is around 85 years old. Are they going to relate to the master of horror? What was I thinking? I love Stephen King stories but will this group? Usually they are into Danielle Steel and the like. Well, I do not like love stories! Let's see what I can do here. This particular book happened to be a collection of short stories, so, as I continued driving, I leafed through the book, (only at red lights of course!) trying to find something that would appeal to my audience. Ah. At the beginning of one of the stories, I found a description of a desolate, wintry snow-covered farm scene. The snow drifted up against the barn walls, and there was almost complete silence. The few remaining weeds of Fall, dried out, rustled against the wind. "How many of you read Danielle Steele", I asked the approximately 125 women. Almost everyone in the room raised her hand. "Well, I'm not going to talk about her today!" Everyone applauded! They had all read the latest from this author, and wanted to hear about something new. "How many of you like books about horror?" One lady raised her hand sheepishly. "Oh, there are some of you here today Well, you will love this latest book by Stephen King. How many of you have heard that name?" A few more responses. I read the paragraph describing the barren landscape scene (dramatically, of course). "Can you see it?," I asked them. "Can you picture the snow and how rich a tapestry Mr. King paints in your mind? "Can you see that the author excels in putting a picture in your thoughts that illustrates what he writes? That is what good writing is all about! That is why Stephen King is considered a master writer," I told the crowd. I concentrated on one small facet of one story in a book of 23 stories, to make a point that would hit home with my audience. You must be able to speak to any audience intelligently, on their level, with information that they will need, or enjoy. Many women approached me after the talk and mentioned that never having read any books of the horror genre, they would give the aforementioned author a try. Now it matters not to me what anybody else in the world reads. Once I am through the door, check in hand, the job is done. Successfully. I made some points, they were accepted. Everyone was happy. See you next time! What are those three most important words? PRACTICE! PRACTICE! PRACTICE! Or, if you prefer, PREPARE! PREPARE! PREPARE! The more you go over your presentation, the more it will become a part of you, By the time you climb the steps to that stage you will be confident that your speech is exactly right for the time, the room, and, most importantly, for your audience.

By the way, don't ever tell your audience that you didn't prepare your speech. They don't know that you didn't, and don't realize exactly how much you know, so go ahead and deliver. Make them think you are the expert on the subject by sounding like you are!

But just wait a minute here. What is Public speaking anyway? Well, I'll tell you what it's not! It's not a big deal! Any communication is just simply getting your point across to whomever it is you are attempting to communicate. It doesn't matter whether it is a joke, a personal experience or a major address to your company's executive staff. Your thoughts are put together in a normal order inside your head until they come out either as written material or spoken words. Normally, proper English is used during this process so there is a common bond between the giver and the receivers of this information. The recipients on the other end of this connection receive this information clearly and are able to understand exactly what it is you are offering, and at this point the information is relayed to either their brain(s) or on paper. That's it! Public speaking is a simple way to transfer information from one person to another. If it's done correctly, succinctly, and in a way that is easily comprehensible you have performed your job. They now know what you wanted them to know. What if you haven't done the job? The general response to your valuable time will be "Huh?"

What constitutes a complete speech? I'll tell you. Here is what you must present when you are called upon to talk to a group. Have you ever prepared a paper for an English Composition class? The first thing you must do is make an opening statement which will allow the reader (or listener) to know exactly what you will be writing (talking) about. It must be a strong statement that will grab the audiences' attention and alert them that this will be a dynamic talk about a dynamic subject. The opening could very well be a question aimed at the audience, especially if the group is small. This will allow the audience to immediately be a part of your discourse, and believe me, you will get their attention because they think you may ask them another question!

"HOW MANY OF YOU THINK THAT WE HAVE A PROBLEM WITH PEOPLE DRIVING WHILE THEY ARE DRUNK"? Maybe this could be even more of an eye opener: "HOW MANY OF YOU HAVE TAKEN JUST ONE MORE LITTLE DRINK ("DON'T WORRY, I'VE DONE THIS A MILLION TIMES"!), BEFORE YOU GET INTO YOUR CAR

AND DRIVE HOME?" You are not looking for anyone in the audience to answer the question, but you do want to pause here to give the question time to sink into their minds. The more personal you can make your subject, short of naming names, the more your audience will feel you are speaking directly to each one of them.

Now you've made your point. You need to expand on that statement to tell your audience that you are not just unhappy about this situation; you are going to offer solutions to end, or at least lessen, the incidence of accidents caused by intoxicated drivers. What are you going to do about it? Here's where you tell them. Give them a few ideas that you think will solve the problem, or describe the situation as you mentioned in the opening statement. The usual number of ideas is three. Just tell them as if they were on a list. Now, the people listening to you have an idea about how you really feel.

THERE ARE MANY WAYS TO PREVENT THIS EVIL AND DANGEROUS PRACTICE! TODAY I WILL OFFER THREE IDEAS WHICH WILL ENABLE DRIVERS WHO OBEY THE LAW TO FEEL, AND ACTUALLY BE, SAFE! At this point, you need to convince them that this is the way to go. Starting at the first idea, explain as fully, simply, and succinctly as possible, each of the three ideas. You should know up front how much time you have for completing your speech, and here is where you do the most tailoring.

"I WILL NOW EXPLAIN THIS FURTHER. MY FIRST IDEA, DA DA, WILL MEAN.......Here is your paragraph or three to expound on this idea, AND THIS IDEA ONLY! THE SECOND IDEA I MENTIONED, DE DUM, ...Continuing in the same vein as number one, sticking to the subject. LASTLY, NUMBER THREE, TRA LA, ... Adding your last "story of the idea" as the last two. So you've told them the premise of the story, and you've expounded on it. As mentioned earlier, here is where you can cut and paste. (I love computers!) Depending on your audience and how much time there is to speak, the middle part, or the body of the speech is the best part to add information or cut some out. You may find, over time, that you have given the same speech to many different groups, plus or minus some lines or even a paragraph or two. Who will know? Remember, you are the only person who knows what you will be speaking about. Never tell them what you forgot, or left out. They don't know! With careful editing, you own half a dozen speeches!

What's next? Perhaps the hardest part of giving a speech is knowing when to end it. Many times I have listened to a great speech only to watch the speaker stammer and stutter, looking all around for help, because he didn't know how to stop. You stop by applying a brake. After you have explained the secrets of life, you must add a strong ending statement to sum up everything you have said. Again, the statement should be strong and concise, wrap up the whole ball of wax, and allow you to end at that point. I'm sure you've heard the expression, "To sum up"...." or "in conclusion"..." and realized that most times, the talk goes on and on. When you apply the brake, step on it and definitively end the talk. "I firmly believe"....." is a line that will allow you to make a final statement, turn to the moderator, and return control of the show over to him/her. OK, that's the very basic run through on presenting a speech. Let's try one. Since we're making up a speech I'll say here that this does not necessarily reflect my true feelings on the subject discussed, although sometimes I wonder. Since we've already addressed the subject of people who are not acting in their own best interest, not to mention the innocent victims who happen to cross their path, let us stay on subject. Use it if you like. Feel free to make changes. Here we go!

Stop driving drunk! How many of you drink at parties, get behind the wheel of your car, and drive yourself and your spouse home? How many of you think this is not a big deal? Well I'm not going to quote you a lot of statistics because you know all the facts. Drunk driving kills! We must come to our senses and join together to stop this insane habit that destroys lives and families.

One of the ways we can do this is to set up surprise inspection stops along streets and highways to test motorists. The second recommendation I proffer is to more deeply ingrain the idea about drunk driving to everyone through increased radio and television announcements. Third, we must make our laws stronger and enforce them to the fullest extent. I know some people will complain about having to stop and submit to a sobriety test in the middle of a thoroughfare, and some might even claim it is unlawful. But those that do imbibe might have second thoughts about drinking at all or driving after having had a few shots. Is it worth lives to try radical ideas? Next, we must get schools, churches, newspapers, tv, radio, any media or forum, to increase the educating of everyone that drinking and driving do not mix. It is wrong! It will kill! We need to stop! Information is the key. Lastly, we cannot let anyone off the hook who kills, maims, or merely harms any other person however slightly. We've got to throw the book at them, and we need to make the book extra heavy! I know you feel the same way I do about this dreadful situation, and I also know you want to help stop it. Think about these ideas. Put them to work. Contact your representatives and tell them how you feel. Together we can stop this senseless, thoughtless, slaughtering. Mr. Moderator!" Of course this was an over simplified scenario that was just put together to make the point. I chose a hot topic that always affects a crowd no matter how large or small. Realize that if you concentrate on speaking about things that normally raise your blood pressure 10 degrees, you're going to be a great success at speaking because your belief will be translated into the energy that will flow from the stage right into and around your audience. Just be sure to keep in control so your blood pressure level doesn't really fly away!

Thinking about blood pressure reminds me of another situation which should cement the issue; namely, knowing what to say and how to say it implies that you CAN say it! Huh? Another most important rule about public speaking is this: never bite off more than you can chew! Once, during a speaking competition, a friend of mine attempted to relate a tale concerning a soldier's letter to his father. The soldier was in Viet Nam, and the time was that week in January when we celebrate the birthday of Dr. Martin Luther King, Jr. The writer mourned the loss of the great humanitarian but was also distraught over the death, the previous day, of his Army buddy, who just happened to be a black man. "Who grieves for Jake, and for how long?", was the central theme of this somber story. Midway through the speech, my friend sobbed, his shoulders shaking convulsively. He paused, trying to gain control of himself enough to finish. The audience, about 100 people, looked around. Everyone seemed nervous, there was a palpable air of uncertainty. Some even looked at me, imploringly, as if to say, "Do something, we're embarrassed!" What could I do? After an interminable delay, my friend was finally able to catch his breath, stop crying, and settled down. He continued his story and concluded it. He received a nice round of applause but we all knew that the applause was more for feeling than for his delivery. Needless to say, my friend was not a finalist in the competition. He's a great guy, a good speaker, and certainly compassionate. But compassion has its place. This incident gave me a great example of what NOT to do. It's best not to dwell on negatives, but the point has been made. If you can't deliver the talk, don't take on the task. You will be uncomfortable, the audience will be uncomfortable, and a great opportunity for you will be lost. Never, never put yourself in this position.

Remember, when you are at the podium, you are in command. All eyes are on you, and you need to reflect this command. This is not to say that one should not talk about points of view with which one does not agree. I've always advocated looking at both sides of the question. Imagine debating an issue you are against! When you study the opposing viewpoints you become more knowledgeable in the subject, because you can answer any questions that may arise. You are the expert! You are in command! Get out there and make your point, forcefully, with style and commitment! I cannot overemphasize the importance of being in total command of whatever subject it is that you will present. Sometimes what you have prepared to speak, however, may not be what you wind up delivering. That is not the usual situation but again, you must be able to perform in a manner that will please the audience. Remember, the show must go on. Also remember, you do want to do this again, assuming you're doing this for payment. Even if your boss asked (commanded) you to deliver this report, address, statement, you need to deliver it perfectly, simply because you will be the center of attraction and you want to convey the notion that not only do you know what you're talking about, but that you can talk about it well.

A year or two ago, a friend invited me to be a guest speaker at his club, made up mostly of engineers. When I asked him about what my subject would be, he told me not to worry about it, just to prepare a few jokes to tell over dinner. It seemed that this evenings' festivities, along with dinner and a band, would include an installation of new officers. When I arrived, Vince introduced me to the outgoing president, who gave me a program for the evening. I noted that I would be introducing both the old group of officers and the new one! I asked if it were possible for me to meet the people involved so I could do a proper presentation, but the soon to be ex-president said that it wasn't necessary! I couldn't very well complain, so I resumed my seat at the head table and watched as the proceedings went on without me. When a lady (ex-president) sat down next to me, I asked her when I would be called upon to speak. She told me not to worry. After a few moments she leaned over to me and asked if I would speak during the serving of the salad. I asked her what she wanted me to speak about, and she again told me not to worry! Salad came and went, and still I sat, wondering just what my role would be. I, of course, had a long list of humorous stories to tell, but as time flew by I continued to question my ability to relate to this crowd. Suddenly, during dessert, my host leaned over and asked me to start speaking to the group. I again asked as to the subject of my talk and she replied, "anything you want!" Whoa! Give me a break! But then I listened. The turning point of all this, as you may guess, was the introduction. Among other superlatives rained upon me, the person who called me to the lectern said: "Mr. Gold has also formally instructed county employees in the fine art of public speaking." Given this opening, I gathered my wits on my way to the speakers' position and opened with, "Good evening, ladies and gentlemen, while relating what meager information I own on speaking in public, I often tell true stories which I hope will relate to the subject at hand, and one of those tales goes like this:...." After that opening, I could tell virtually anything I wanted; the field was open and I could run anywhere I chose. Because I was speaking to a professional group, the smooth continuity between the master of ceremonies and me was critical, and it worked out perfectly. What I had prepared was right for the occasion and, just as important, had seamlessly kept the program running as though I'd spoken to this crowd many times.

So, being totally aware of your subject being most imperative, knowing HOW to present your subject is important as well. Once you have become adept at speaking in public, you will learn how to accomplish this, but, like anything else, it will require time, effort, and experience.

Remember that when you are asked to deliver a presentation, it is YOU who is being asked. What does that mean? One does not become another person simply because he/she is relaying some information and happens to do so at the front of the room, no matter how large that room happens to be. Do people actually change when delivering a speech? Read this!

Back in the days when I was a student at Dale Carnegie, a 17 week course of self improvement, I was elected by my classmates to return to the next course as a graduate assistant. I remained an assistant for a total of 3 courses. The main requirement of the GA's was to give sample speeches to the class (about 40 students) to show the proper way to deliver a speech on anger, happiness, and other assorted mind clearing topics. There were four GA's for each class. One of the GA's who had assisted during my initial training session and other classes, was a likeable guy named Rob. Rob was recently out of law school and was getting ready to hang his shingle. I noticed that whenever Rob was called upon to deliver a talk, a change took place. Now we, as GA's, sat in the back of the room, behind the class, and when called, one of us would stride to the front of the room, face the group and deliver a dynamic two minute presentation. To my great interest, I noticed that when Rob stood up, and started on his way to the podium, he seemed to be a shrinking violet. His shoulders were drooped over, his head dropped down as though he were searching the floor for buried treasure. Rob was not smiling. Approaching the halfway point, however, an amazing physical change occurred!

Rob's shoulders became squared, the head raised and became erect, eyes turned toward the instructor. Before our eyes, Rob changed from Clark Kent to Superman! He reached the podium, turned to face the audience, his entire demeanor happy and confident as his words leaped across the room and electrified all ears. Rob had donned the "CLOAK OF SPEAKERDOM" (I created that phrase!), while taking 50 steps to the front of the room. At this point Rob was the best speaker in the world, at least in his mind, which was all that counted at the time. He commanded attention from everyone. When the speech was completed, rousing applause accompanied Rob during his trek to the back of the room, while his shoulders dropped a bit, and the search for buried treasure resumed. I do realize that each and every one of us has his or her own way of coping with a situation. When it comes to delivering a speech however, I'm going to let you in on a little secret.

When you are speaking, you don't become someone else. Unless you are an actor or actress, portraying another person, you are ALWAYS yourself and must act accordingly, no pun intended! If you can talk to friends in the hallway, you can talk to anyone because there is no difference! Remember, communication is just that. You are only exchanging ideas. It is YOUR idea! Talk about it! If you can air those ideas so they can be understood, you have done what you were supposed to do. You are a Communicator!

While I am on, (or near) the subject, I will tell you about a friend of mine, Paul Finizio, who was instrumental in motivating me enough to persue a public speaking career. One of the best attorneys in town, (and who could speak better than THOSE guys?) Paul was the instructor during my four tours of Dale Carnegie Courses. He was then, and still is, a great motivator and teacher. He is always "up", and never fails to inspire anyone he meets. At the same time, Paul was also the president of a local

Toastmaster's International club. This organization exists for the sole purpose of increasing one's skill in the fine art of public speaking.

Upon my graduation from the Dale Carnegie course, Paul invited me to attend a meeting of his Toastmasters' club, held every week at an upscale restaurant. I will be describing my earlier experiences at the club later, but for now, back to Paul. I caught up with him at a party a few weeks ago. When he saw me he yelled out my name and virtually ran to me with both hands outstretched. He always makes you feel so important! Paul is one of the best speakers I have ever heard, if not the best. Because of his ability to communicate well and motivate others, he has all the confidence needed to accomplish anything he sets his mind to do. You, too, can accomplish anything you want, just like Paul. There is no secret. If you can stand up in front of any size group of people, speak to them clearly and effectively and tell them what they want to hear, you will HAVE to be motivated! You will HAVE to be confident! That's all there is to it.

Have you ever played baseball? Golf? Gone bowling? What's this got to do with public speaking? A lot. Have you ever played baseball, gone through the experience of standing at the plate and visualize the pitcher throwing the ball, you seeing it clearly, you swinging the bat right into the path of the ball, hitting it past and over everyone? Have you had the pleasure of seeing, just before swinging the golf club, hitting that little ball, watching the flight of that ball towards the cup, watching it bounce once and roll towards that cup? There's a name for that. It's called positive imaging. I sincerely hope that you have not had the opposite thought when you were about to complete a task. You thought to yourself "I'll never be able to do it. I'm just not capable of finishing". Guess what: if you think you can't finish the job, you won't. You must be positive in all aspects of your life, not to mention a new skill such as public speaking. You must be able to picture yourself confidently strolling to the lectern, a minimum of notes in your hand, standing squarely in front of your audience, smiling at them, radiating confidence, delivering a strong and well rehearsed talk. Upon returning to your seat, hearing the beautiful sound of thunderous applause filling the air, and most importantly, filling your ears, the knowledge that you have succeeded, that you have delivered. You must see this before it happens. You must think successfully. You have thought it out. You have written it down. You have rewritten it countless times. You have edited and shortened it, making it more concise. You have reduced your information to notes. You have further reduced your notes to a series of key words that require only a glance at the card in your hand, or resting on the lectern, so the audience can readily see that the presentation is not being read to them. You have practiced. And practiced. The hard work is over. It's all downhill from here. You're a public speaker!

Here's what's written in every book you've ever read on the subject of public speaking. It's also in every book you haven't read on the subject so I'll save you the time of reading those.

"So you've been asked to speak! Congratulations! You are going to be the center of attention! You will command the respect of all those who listen to you!" So on and so on.

Do you have a problem with those statements? I hope not. They are basically true. You might ask yourself who these people are that assume you have the potential to make a fool of yourself. These people are, for the most part, professional speakers who have not one iota of fear about standing before any size group of people and delivering their talk. If they do have a fear, you have to give them a lot of credit for faking it! You wonder what will happen to you after stumbling on your words, and failing miserably at your mission. You have the wrong mind-set here, my friends. How many football, baseball, or basketball games have you watched. How many ballets? Ever want to do any or all of those things? Did you ever think you could accomplish any of those feats you observed? Maybe so, because, as you must be aware, these events are achieved only after long hard preparation and training, in most cases over years of work. Guess what. All of us, physical problems notwithstanding, can speak. The great majority of us can speak with a pretty fair comprehension of our language, so that anyone listening to us can understand what it is we are saying. So the concept you must believe is this: the only difficulty you have in your mind about public speaking IS IN YOUR MIND! What will be the reaction you receive upon concluding your talk? Well, after you have determined the topic, the length of the time required to complete the talk, noted the size and layout of the room, realized the number and type of the audience, actually written and practiced, practiced, practiced your speech, TA DA, the hard part is over! Remember that. The hard work is over. It's true. By the time you get to the podium, look around that room and smile, you are the expert in the subject you will discuss. It can't be any other way. You volunteered, or were chosen to do this, and it was your responsibility to complete the task, and the finished product, as in anything else, is directly proportionate to the amount of work expended on it. What will be the reaction you receive upon concluding your talk? Assuming you've done all these things required before the presentation, your audience will be completely tuned to your words. They will listen, raptly, waiting for your next idea. Because everything was thought out and presented in a logical order, it made sense and was easily comprehended by your listeners. What happens upon the conclusion of all this is the standing ovation you receive. That's the only result that can occur, because you have done your homework and you have proven it!

When I was an instructor for Broward County, Florida, I conducted classes in public speaking. They were daylong sessions and in the first few hours I would try to instill the fact that it was so easy to talk to a group, anyone could do it! The class, about 25 people, would be divided into groups of three or four, and each student would deliver a three minute speech to the other members of the group. After lunch, a good time to reflect on what they had accomplished, the group reassembled into one group and then delivered the same speech to the entire class. By this time, it was thought, they were on their way, a few steps, at least, to conquering that great fear. Now came the time for one particular class member to stand up and regale us with her talk. She had done well in the smaller group. I had circulated throughout the room during the first presentations to note any particular problems, or, mostly, to show support by nodding and smiling. During this ladies' talk, she even had the presence of mind to smile back! She approached the dais, looking somewhat sheepish. She stood erect, looked out over the crowd.....and started to cry. "I can't do this!" she exclaimed, running out of the room. I immediately instructed the class to take a fifteen minute break while I attempted to calm her down. I looked around the area but could not locate her. Finally, after ten minutes, she came out of the ladies' room, her eyes dried. She saw me and said that she could not continue with the class. It was "too much for me", she said. I brought her back into the classroom but no amount of prodding could bring her back to the front of the room. I promised to hold her hand but that did not work either. I felt as bad as she did. My first failure. It had never occurred to me that this would happen. I always thought about her whenever I presented a class.

Two years later, at yet another class, I notice a familiar face. There she was, in the first seat, right up front. When she stood to introduce herself, a requirement in my classes, she said this was her second attempt at this class, but would explain later. Came the time for her to assume the position at the front of the room and before she had a chance to speak, I noticed the other three members of her group whisper to others things like, "Listen to this, it's gonna be good." Her four minute speech was the story of what happened to her at the previous class. She mentioned that she would never put herself in a position where she could not get out gracefully. She noted that with the proper mind-set, she could accomplish anything, and so could YOU, she pointed out to the rest of the class. It was one of the best speeches I had ever heard and the class must have felt the same way, given the applause that followed the lady to her seat. She taught us all a valuable lesson that day, one I will never forget. Congratulations to her, and a thank you as well!

While we're on the subject of what to talk about, remember that virtually all the talks I give come from true events that have happened to me. Two things occur when I do this. First, they are true, so I do not have to tax myself thinking up stories to talk about. Usually, a so-called homespun story is very interesting, simply because it is real and may strike a chord with some of the listeners. Second, because it is a true story, I do not have to stretch my brain trying to remember long speeches. All I need to do is think about the things that have happened to me. Sometimes I start off a speech with these words. "Those of you who have heard me speak know I do not give speeches; I tell stories!" This is an opening that informs the audience that they are going to hear a story, not a dry, memorized list of facts that may lull them to sleep. While I am talking about stories here, I will also tell you that I often try to tack on a moral or two at the end of those stories. The moral can be serious, or a great way to finish with humor, but they always accomplish one thing.-they end a story. Here is an example-a story of near tragedy, great excitement, and, oh, never mind. Check this out.

Once upon a time, a long time, when I was about ten years old, a classmate and I decided to get on the trolley car, ride "uptown", and watch a fellow student perform in a children's play. It was a morning show, on a Saturday, and when the show was over, my friend and I decided to visit a nearby penny arcade. Our respective parents had trusted us with an extra dollar or two. (In those days it really was a penny arcade, so two dollars was a windfall!) After playing virtually every game in the place, we soon got bored and thought about our next move-the movies! My friend was very excited about the re-release of King Kong, which was being shown at the theater next door. Now, back in those days, I could not watch horror movies, even if the monster was just an overgrown ape. I was not going into that movie theater! My friend was adamant, so I left him with Kong, and went to see another movie. Later, when the movie was finished (I do not recall what I saw), I found, to my dismay, I had no money. Too much pin-ball, I guess. Well, I was a bright fellow. I knew what to do. I went to the nearest street corner and called to the policeman who was on duty there. A policeman was always on duty at the intersections in those days.

I explained my situation to the officer and told him that I would gladly mail back to him the fifteen cents he would loan me so I would be able to return home. He told me not to worry about the money and asked where I lived. “2500 Marshall Street”, I replied, leaving out the most important part, the SOUTH designation. The officer then sent me to the proper corner (he thought) to await the trolly car. Unfortunately, the policeman assumed I lived in the 2500 block of NORTH Marshall street! As instructed, when I boarded the trolly, I asked the conductor to let me know when we arrived at the 2500 block, then picked a seat near him. I certainly did not want to miss the call. Sometime later, I heard him exclaim, “2500”! I thanked him and got off the trolly. I looked around at all the porches. There were no porches in my neighborhood! Walking the once normal block to Marshall Street, I felt as though I had entered the Twilight Zone! That was very strange in itself: the Twilight Zone had not been invented yet!

Where was I? What had happened? I walked for what seemed hours. I was lost, all right. I had no idea that I was fifty blocks from my home. Five miles! I found myself on a corner dominated by a tall building with a long, wide curving set of steps in front of it. I climbed a few of those steps, sat down, wrapped my head in my arms and cried like a baby. After awhile, I realized that someone was tooting a car horn at me. (There was no one else around). I looked up and saw a taxi cab driver waving his hand out of the car window at me. “Hey kid, are you lost?” I sobbed at him. “Yes, I am.” He motioned me to the cab and asked me another question. "Is your father's name Victor?" I was stunned. Yes, my father's name WAS Victor. How did he know? I stammered my reply to him, and the driver told me to get into the cab. I did, and the cabbie told me he knew my father and would take me home. When we arrived at my house, my folks were so glad to see me they forgot to yell at me for not calling home earlier in the day, but my dad also told me that because I looked so much like him, someone recognized me as being his son. As a further stroke of luck, the friend did not even charge us for the ride! It was great to be home. There are two morals to this story; you should look like your father and know a lot of cab drivers!

Notice that the three point writing style I described previously is not used in this story, but when a personal story is told, the natural flow of the story unfolds as the events are brought out point by point. There is a logical step by step order to the speech. In either case, you must be sure that the road you travel during your talk is straight and to the point. The fact of the matter is, I can not over-emphasize knowing your subject. How do the Boy Scouts feel about it? BE PREPARED!

You should always keep in mind that almost everything that happens to you, or that you know about, will make for a very interesting talk, if you construct it correctly. People love to hear about real things that have happened to real people. Take lots of notes when you are involved in a human interest event. Now, here is another story to illustrate something that will rarely happen to you. At least I hope not!

Some time ago I was a stock broker and on one particular morning delivered a talk about stocks and bonds to a group of older citizens: the men's club of a large condo association in South Florida. The standard deal for brokers speaking to potential customers was this: I would pay for breakfast, which consisted of eggs, toast and coffee, and they would listen to what I had to say. The bill amounted to a little over three hundred dollars, but if I managed to open a few accounts, I would more than make up for the expense. Anyway, here I was, up on stage (one of my favorite places) finishing a forty five minute talk. I asked for questions from the audience but there was not a murmur. No one stirred. "Come on", I implored, "someone must have a question." No one moved. "Well, folks, this leads me to believe one of two things. Either I have explained myself so well there are no possible questions, or I've gone so far over your heads, you have no idea about what to ask me." Actually, I realized again the fear of speaking in public-on their behalf of course! If someone had a question, he may not want to stand up in a crowd to ask it! "So what Im going to do is this: I'm going to come down off this stage, sit down, and enjoy this wonderful breakfast that your fellow club members have prepared. However, I want you to know that if you do have a question, please, please, feel free to interrupt me, even if my mouth is full. I am here for that purpose only, so take advantage of me. It is my pleasure to be here." With that having been said, I sat down at the table provided for me and began to eat. A short time passed and an old, bent, bearded gentleman approached my table and stood before me. "Yes sir, is there anything I may do for you?" "Mr. Gold, I have a question for you. "I'll be very happy to answer it for you, sir. What is your question?" "Mr. Gold, are you going to finish that bagel??!!"

Rarely, as I have stated earlier, will you experience an event similar to this one. Obviously, in an environment where some, if not all, of the audience is captive, your talk will bounce off deaf ears. Turning a minus into a plus, however, is easy. I opened a few accounts, made some new friends, and had the added enjoyment of doing what I like best, speaking in front of an audience. The humor of the event did not escape me, either. Another benefit, of course, was the realization that I gained another true to life adventure that I could relate to others. Given this is the worst case scenario, notice, no tomatoes or eggs were thrown at me. Just a poor soul only interested in his belly, which, by the way, was not heard to growl during the delivery of my speech. In all my years of public speaking, this was truly the only time someone gave a negative reply to a talk of mine.

And he didn't even realize he did it! When you speak to a captive audience, make the best of it. Try a little humor. Although everybody cannot be happy all the time, try to make it so when you are in charge. Radiate your strength and your willingness to be in this position, and it will transfer to your audience. It will! Believe me. So don't worry about how your listeners seem to feel. Know it, do it, damn the torpedoes, as they say, and fire away. You will be a hit!

Remember, you will be talking to everyone in the room. If you cannot look at each person in the room because of the sheer number of them, you must scan the room, taking in as much area as possible. Audiences are much more responsive to someone who is talking directly to them. This will become second nature to you after you have gotten some speeches under your belt. Trust me.

Suppose you are walking in a hallway and some friends approach you. You start a conversation. Do you have a problem with this scenario? Of course not. Let us suppose now that there are six people around you, some of them your friends. Do you experience any difficulty in speaking with them and making your point? Okay, so far. Now, imagine those six people are all standing in front of you. Having a problem yet? I would not think so. It is the same group. Now, let us get some chairs and have these people sit down in front of you. Can you still speak to them clearly, making your point? What is the difference now? It is only that you are a little taller than the rest because you are standing and they are sitting. What else has changed? Were they listening to you before they were sitting? Are they still aware of what it is you are saying? Hey, a few other people were passing by and, having heard your topic have stopped and are now listening to you as well. Having an anxiety attack yet? How come? You must be making sense because more people are becoming interested in what you have to say. There are about ten or eleven people standing and/or sitting in front of you, and the only difference between them and you is that you are doing all the talking. If someone asks you a question, will you answer? Of course you will. Why is that? Because you know what you are talking about. Even if the subject is the game or TV show you watched last night, you know everything about it, so you can speak with confidence. So what is the big deal? There isn't any. Let us make one more change. Let us put you up on a stage and the ten or eleven people right there in the front row. (OK, you can have a lectern if you really want!) What is the difference now? Of course. You are now much taller than you were before! You have to look down at the people to whom you are speaking. The only other difference is, you have something to say, and you are saying it! That is all. You have no super powers. You are able to do what any human being can do. Talk. Easy, isn't it? Just a little conversation between friends. This is the only way to look at public speaking. You are always among friends. You just seem to have a little bit more knowledge which you want to share with your friends. They are happy to be listening to you because they will be learning something from you. This is why the speaker never thanks the audience. Oh, you didn't know that, did you? The audience, theoretically, should thank the speaker (and they do, through their applause) since they will be gaining valuable knowledge from the speaker. The only time a speaker should thank a group is when he or she receives a check or an award. Or dinner! Got it?

You know, a good way to relate to your audience is to arrive at your destination early enough to mingle with the crowd. This assumes, of course, that the situation exists that allows you to do this, such as an open bar before dinner, or the like. A lot of insight as to the mood of your audience will be gained if you simply talk to them in normal conversation. Just in case your talk is controversial, by having previously listened and noting the general mood of the people, you can possibly tune your speech to suit the situation. In addition, just imagine you are in the audience, asking a question, and the moderator, or speaker, responds to you personally, i.e., using your name! Does this make a greater impression on you? You bet. How did the speaker get to know your name? Oh yes, you spoke with him earlier, before the meeting came to order. Now you're back on the stage. Don't ever ask the audience a question when you don't know the answer yourself! If you act like you don't know what you're talking about, that's the way the audience will perceive you, and all respect, not to mention your command of them, will be lost.

Being in command of the audience reminds me also that there are two basic schools of thought concerning standing at the lectern. The speaker is also in command of that! Some veteran speakers say that the speaker should never leave the lectern unattended. This means that the person introducing a speaker stands behind the lectern until the speaker, who has been approaching the front of the room during his introduction, shakes hands and STANDS BEHIND the lectern, taking control. During the last line or two of the talk, when the emcee realizes the speech is over, he/she heads toward the lectern, TO TAKE CHARGE again. The handshake, on either side of the speech, is the defining moment, when command changes from one to another. Conversely, the other school of thought is that once a speaker has taken control of the festivities, he/she is free to wander all over the stage, or, if possible, to enter into the seating area while speaking. The speaker must be back at the lecture when the talk is completed, of course. Where do I stand on this question? Whatever makes you happy. When you become a polished speaker, you will command respect and attention wherever you speak. Since you are just "talking to friends," be at ease, and make it fun.

Speaking (ha ha) of being at ease, here's another bit of information for you. There is no rule that says you cannot stop, take a breath, sip some water, or just look around. This can accomplish more than a few things. It allows you time to think about the next part of your presentation. Following an important idea, it gives the audience time to digest the facts. The audience will be more relaxed seeing that you are taking the time to relax as well. As a matter of fact, when you want to make a point, there are other ways to do so besides raising your voice. A moment of silence after a heavy statement will give the audience time to digest that piece of information and understand that it was an important item, one they need to retain. During that rare moment when you feel panic about the next thing you have to say, stop, look around, take a drink from that glass there on the lectern. It's there for you. While you drink and look around, calm down. Think about what you're talking about, and what comes next. It'll be there. Believe me. I'm tellin' ya!

Just as a change of pace, I will now mention a few thoughts about a very rare occurrence. Here are some ideas on how to deal with disruptive people. First you must keep in mind that there are different levels of disruption. For example, someone making a comment to the person sitting next to him/her during your presentation, as opposed to a person continually talking during your speech. But none of you have had these problems have you? The overall answer to the problem is two-fold. Eliminate the problem but keep the person! In the first example, that of a simple comment or statement, the question I ask myself is: Did the incident disrupt the audience enough so that I've lost the attention of the group? If that is the case, you must bring the focus back to yourself with an appropriate statement, without, of course, insulting the guilty party. In the second example, the constant talker, you, as the speaker have two choices. You can publicly recognize the offense and the offender, or not. By making a statement such as "sir/madam, I will be pleased to speak with you about your (argument, concerns, etc) immediately after my presentation. Please let me continue," You are focusing attention away from you. If you must use this approach, Quickly get the audience back with an appropriate statement such as: moving right along, or, I will now reiterate the points covered earlier. This may be an ideal time for a joke, depending on the time you have and your subject. Not everyone can accomplish this, so if you don't feel comfortable doing it, don't! Of course when directly confronting someone in the audience, you run the risk of alienating the person, causing either an escalation of the disruption, or worse, causing the person to leave. You do not want to do that! Try to ride out the storm, and finish your talk. At the proper time (preferably before the person leaves that particular meeting, and it is a regularly held meeting), you should speak to the individual p r i v a t e l y! Explain, calmly, how his/her actions affects not only the speaker, but the audience as well, pointing out that a major part of communicating, is listening. Never use a loud abusive manner in attempting to correct anyone. Try, instead, to remember that communication is a mutually supportive condition. We must all assist, teach and learn, together. If the problem persists, even after your discussion, you may consider asking a mediator, perhaps the group's president, to step in and talk to the offender. Again, and foremost, always keep in mind that this particular goal of the organization to whom you are speaking is to listen and comprehend whatever it is you are saying, and how you communicate your concerns to the offender will go a long way in conveying to that audience that you care very much about your end of the deal and you would hope that the deal was completed at their end! Do not take these interruptions personally! Handle them correctly, continuing to strive to better yourself as you go. Do not quit!!

You know what else is important? Looking sincere as well as being sincere, although I don't know if you can have one without the other. Sometimes, during my classes, one of my students will be delivering a speech (ALL of my students speak!), and it will supposedly be a passionate speech. The problem is, the speaker doesn't

LOOK passionate! How convincing does a speaker seem, talking about a maddening situation, while smiling? Not too convincing, I would say. One needs to control emotions, especially during a talk, but one also needs to let the emotion through enough so the audience will feel the complete sincerity of you, the speaker. I will ask the student to repeat at least part of the talk adding some sort of action, such as banging on the lectern, to make the feeling real. If you feel it, the audience will, too. When I was an assistant at Dale Carnegie, at one session, each student was given a rolled up newspaper and was instructed to pound on the lectern while speaking on the subject, "Do you know what really makes me mad?" There were lots of red faces and plenty of sweat at the end of that night, but the students learned that when a speech of passion is given, passion must be felt, by the speaker, and then by the audience. That's another reason why practicing is so very important. The more you study your talk, the more control and mastery you will have over it. Not only will you be in command of the audience, you'll be in command of yourself.

Once upon a time, hey, there's a catchy opening, I was preparing to speak to a group of people, and I had an hour to do some book reviews. I've done many of these, and, since I love to read, why shouldn't I capitalize on it? I never do best sellers. My audiences usually have already read the top ten list books. I just pick out six or seven stories that I have enjoyed reading and then try to convince the people to whom I speak, that they should read them as well.

One particular book used very blunt and colorful language, especially during the first few chapters, since the beginning of the story happened to take place in a maximum security penitentiary. As we've learned, certain types of speeches are not received warmly by certain audiences. When starting to discuss this particular novel, however, I merely mentioned the location of the opening. This set the tone of the book. As the story continued with the eventual breakout from the prison by three of the main subjects of the story, and their many skirmishes with other central figures, I explained how this book dealt with relationships, between the men themselves, between the cops and their wives, and eventually between the police and the fugitives. Instead of talking about some of the more lurid passages, I focused on the characters themselves, staying away from the nasty words and phrases, and making it easy for myself to close this section of my talk. The easy ending was this: "This is a book full of shoot-em-ups and passion, but here's a little warning. Fight your way past the dirty talk in the beginning and you'll be rewarded with a great story with an exciting finish." What does this have to do with anything? As you become more proficient in speaking to others, BY SPEAKING TO OTHERS, you will learn how to use words and phrases to suit the mood of your audience, and swing their thoughts around to agree with your own. This means that you will have the power to change other people's ideas, at least for the time being. For example, some of the people in the audience just discussed might very well pick up a copy of the aforementioned book and make an attempt to read it. They might not get past the first few lurid pages, but at least they made an effort, and the effort was affected by you! Imagine how your mastery of your own language will increase. You will have the ability to use words that, as of now, are unknown to you! In addition, you will be able to make people understand what it is you are trying to tell them because of this ability. You will be able to turn negatives into positives. You will have the power to put your own ideas into other people! What a power that is!

All you need to do is to know what you're going to say and how you are going to say it! Here it comes: Practice, Practice, Practice!

Strive, however, to be understood by your audience, not only in the usage of your words but why and how they are used. For example, when short sentences are used, the audience will grasp an idea more quickly. Remember that! IT WILL WORK! Understand the concept? You would not want to create a speech using only short sentences. Mix in sentences which are longer, to add substance and description to your story.

Do not forget adverbs and adjectives, those words which will increase the action and enhance the richness of the picture you are painting with language. Spread out the major, hard hitting points of your objective, as formulated earlier. You do not want to put all your big guns up front and push your talk downhill from that point. Conversely, saving the critical lines for the ending section may create some yawns until you get there! Use key words, repeated, throughout your talk. The audience will listen closer, waiting for those key words. It has happened, quite frequently, that the audience will anticipate those key words, and will actually say them out loud, without cue. When that occurs, you realize you have them in the palms of your hands and they are yours to mold!

At this point, I would like to list some ideas that will lead to good communication. What is wrong with that statement? Think about it. I will give you some time to consider the question. Tick tick tick tick....... OK, I would like to list some ideas. Well, why don't I? Saying you would like to introduce the next speaker (as another example), one might reply to you: go ahead, do it! You must have, at least to start out, a good knowledge of the English language, and you you must make sure you use the right words to convey exactly what it is you want the audience to hear. A better way to start this page would be: At this point, here is a list of ideas.... Or, simply, Here is a list of ideas.... In the case of introductions: "Our next speaker is from Philadelphia, and he/she brings to us a wealth of information". This is a simple statement which accomplishes a few things quite easily, the first of which is to alert the audience to the fact that a new face will soon appear before them. After the topic is mentioned concerning that wealth of information, and any other information that explains who the speaker is and why he/she is present and about to speak, the audience is warmed up to receive this new person who will now be in command of the proceedings. That having been noted, here are some ideas previously touched upon. Know what it is you want to say, and what you want the audience to hear. Realize that you can say these things in a manner clear and meaningful enough so the audience will understand and retain them. Use simple language relative to your audience. Do not use technical jargon (unless you are speaking to technicians) that will not be understood or recognized. On the other hand, do not speak down to the crowd. Know your audience before you speak, and you will be correct in the manner you speak to them. Know where your talk is to be delivered. If possible, visit the room, and test the facilities, so you will know just how loud or soft your voice will have to be so everyone present will be able to hear you. Remember my story about the I.R.S. Know who is sitting out there, and do not offend anyone. Tailor your speech to reflect the mood of the audience, and you will be able to stir their passions! Make sure your speech is not double entendre unless you mean to keep them guessing about where you are coming from, or you are delivering a humorous talk. Will there be a question and answer period? This should be determined initially when you discuss your presentation with the person in charge. Adequate time should be set aside to accomplish this, and this will be a part of the total time allotted to you. Definitely, know the answers, too! End the speech when it is finished. Someone once said: (my apologies to whomever it was!) "It is my job to speak to you for awhile, and it is your job to listen to me. I hope we finish at the same time!" Be sincere. That pretty much says it all. Be at ease. They have come to listen to you. They want to know what you have to say. Tell them and be at ease while you do so!

Are you keeping an ear on your vocal delivery? Is your voice being heard all the way to the back of the room? If you are mad, does your voice convey the feeling? Does your voice convey sincerity? If not, make it so. Your voice is the interface (I'm into computers) between your thoughts and your audience. Make sure it delivers. Are you using the right words? Have you checked out the type of people that are your audience? Are they technically oriented? Are they a group of people that have no idea about the subject you are or will be discussing? Will you offend any ONE of them by saying the wrong thing? Choose your words carefully!

Eye contact helps your audience feel like they are a part of the proceedings. There may be a stadium full of listeners, but you are still looking left, right, first row, last row, and every possible seating area in between, all the time. It is imperative that you are attempting to involve everyone present by at least looking at them. If they feel involved, they will be involved! Facial expressions are closely related to what you are saying. They should be. A lady in one of my classes started off her talk with this statement: "Do you know what really makes me mad?" SHE WAS SMILING! How do you think the audience reacts to a speaker who is not showing the emotion he/she wants the audience to share? Just as in real life (?), you need to show sincerity when you are speaking, or the person(s) to whom you are speaking will not be able to share the same conviction. Remember that Dale Carnegie class I mentioned earlier? When you are banging ANYTHING on the lectern, it sure makes the point. Take that fist of yours and use it! Another member of one of my classes stood up tall and, as soon as he started to speak, jammed his hands straight down his sides. He was standing at attention! After a minute or two, he realized that this was not the thing to do, so he thrust his hands deep into his pockets, but only for a few seconds before he crossed his arms in front of himself. He next grabbed both sides of the lecturn and hung on for dear life.

In the book, I CAN SEE YOU NAKED, (Ron Hoff, 1988) the author suggests you hold a heavy book in each hand while you are practicing your speech. He notes that only occasionally, because of the added weight, you will use your arms to make a point. These are the arm movements you should commit to your presentation! With all due respect to Mr. Hoff, however, would this not be harder then just acting normally? Please don't waste your time adding anything to your presentation which is not needed. RELAX! Be Yourself! Remember, all you are doing is talking to some friends. There is no need to be uptight. When you are walking down the street you never worry about how your arms are attached to your shoulders; you do not need to worry about that when you are speaking. Be natural. Be yourself. Do it! I insist! Seriously, it is critical that you always, in all endeavors, be yourself. If you can keep that in mind, you will be most successful. Remember that cloak of speakerdom on my friend Rob that I talked about earlier? It never existed.

Recalling the topic of stopping during a talk, possibly drinking a little water, looking around at your audience. How do they look? Are they smiling? I'll bet they are. You can even smile back while you do this. To do this you will need to find an appropriate moment to pause to keep the continuity of your speech. Here is another place to be natural, to be yourself. The only more important point I can emphasize to you is to prepare. I should probably use these two major rules in my title but it would not be snappy or eye-catching enough. Here it is again, though: The main thrust of my little guide. Write this down. That's OK. I will write it for you. BE YOURSELF AND PRACTICE, PRACTICE, PRACTICE.

Last on this list is your energy and motivational level. Look, you have to do this. You are going to do it, and you are going to be good at it, too! You might as well feel as though you are up to the task, and look like it as well. This is a great opportunity for you. Act like it! Go out there with a smile on your face, confidence in your mind, and a message to be heard. But first, learn everything in this book. Then, and only then, (what else would you expect me to say?) will you be a great success.

What is being yourself? Who are you anyway? Here are two more stories which I hope will make it easier for you to be whoever you want to be.

In 1986 I made a move that changed my life. I joined Toastmasters International, a organization made up of many clubs designed to increased one's ability to speak in public. As I mentioned earlier I had attended one of the Dale Carnegie courses (four times) and it happened that the trainer during those sessions was a member of a Toastmasters club which convened not far from my home. I decided to visit a meeting which was held at a downtown restaurant. There were about 25 people present and I watched in amazement at what went on. After a short business meeting something called "Table Topics" started up. I soon learned that this was an exercise in impromptu speaking. A member chosen the previous week, had thought up some questions and asked other members to respond, with no previous notice. The member had to speak on the question for 2 minutes! Even if the respondent had no idea at all about the subject! Imagine my surprise when Paul, my instructor at the prestigious Dale Carnegie, (and attorney par excellence) was called upon to explain his actions as a Hari Krishna member, soliciting funds at an airport! Paul stood, actually twirled around a few times, effected an Eastern Indian accent, and gave a hilarious answer to the question. He never, by the way, insulted anyone or any institution during the full two minutes he acted. I was amazed. How could I compete with this level of competence? I wondered all week if I was capable of this kind of performance. Would I be in over my head? Finally I decided in favor of the old bromide, nothing ventured, nothing gained. I returned the following week.

I was welcomed back eagerly, and, after the usual preliminaries "Table Topics" was started. Since I had not given a check for enrollment I was not yet a member so the "topic master" asked me if I would be willing to try a question. Go ahead, I thought to myself, go for it! I agreed to field a question. "Mr. Gold is here today in his official capacity as Hurricane Awareness Department Director, and he is willing to explain to us today some of the dangers of this horrible storm. Mr. Gold!" One of the great secrets of speaking off the cuff is learning how to commence THINKING while you slooowly rise from your chair. Hurricanes! What do I know about hurricanes beside the fact that they can blow the roof off of your house? Wait a second! Remember last week? I had been living on the beach in Fort Lauderdale, Florida for about 8 months, and just last week had been informed by the condo association that I would have to put up my storm shutters immediately. I thought about those metal sheets, 6 feet high and 3 feet wide. I remember how unwieldy each of them had been as I moved them, one at a time, into position on the outside wall covering my rather large windows. Remembering also that true to life stories are easier to relate, and easier to relate TO, I told that story with a little embellishment. I mentioned that in my capacity as director of the facility, I was checking on these window coverings for a friend, and I was attempting to mount one of these forms to the wall. A sudden gust of wind grabbed the kite-like metal board and, with me holding on for dear life, blew it straight up into the sky. After screaming for a few minutes I realized that I could pretty much steer this "kite" by pressing on one side or the other, and actually became quite adept at flying over the ocean, and then over the city which certainly I was seeing from a new perspective. I was really enjoying the flight, now that I was in control, but starting thinking that people would worry about me, since I was due to attend a party that very night. By careful steering I was able to find my condo and touch down lightly right on my very own balcony, quickly fastening my "kite" to the wall so I wouldn't take off again! As my job is to present solutions to dangers present in such storms, my advice to all of you, I said, is to wear very heavy boots when attempting an installation such as this. I received a standing ovation and won a certificate for the best "table topics" of the evening. I really will never know if I won the award because of my talk or the fact that it was my first talk, but I do know that at that first meeting my confidence soared. I was equal to the task and had proven it! Since that day so many years ago I have won many awards for speaking in public, both in Toastmasters and out, but that particular evening is one I will not soon forget.

I guess I am giving you a commercial break here because I highly recommend Toastmasters International if you truly want to become an excellent public speaker. What better opportunity could exist for you when you find yourself sitting among people who are, or have been in the same situation as yourself? Each of these folks found him/herself with dry mouth and wet hands, standing in front of peers, thinking that tomatoes, eggs, or worse, stones, would soon be flying in his/her direction. BUT IT NEVER HAPPENS!!! Most everyone in the world has experienced these very same fears but again, you are going to defeat those fears by going ahead with your plans to actually do this thing that seems to be so difficult. Guess what, after the first talk, those feelings of insecurity and doubt will lessen just a bit. Everyone will compliment you on your presentation because you were GOOD! The next time you are faced with the prospect of having to deliver a speech, you will want to work a little harder, to make sure that this talk will be better than the last one. You will practice a little longer to insure this. By the time your third speech is awaited, people will be anxious to hear you, and they will be awarded. You will be successful. I guarantee it!

To bounce around a little, there was something else about that Dale Carnegie course I wanted to mention to you. At one of the later classes in the seventeen week course, each student is given a special assignment to complete at that time, and the assignments are generally looked upon as being something less than necessary. For example, one of the assignments, or "skits", was to assume the role of a circus high diver, standing at the top of a very high pole, about to dive into a glass of water! Chairs are placed in a large circle so you have to stand in the middle of your classmates, pretend you are the ringmaster down on the ground, introducing the diver, then pretend you are the diver, and simulate jumping from a high tower. Once you land in that little glass of water (sploosh, you are required to say) you jump up, twirl around and hum a little circus-like ditty. Everyone does laugh, but each class member is prepared to receive the response. There are other dramas that any graduate of Dale Carnegie will recognize, but the question remains, why are you forced to play this seemingly foolish game?

Remember that whatever you do in life, you need to do it the very best way that you can. When you have performed this feat, you will gain instant knowledge that, if you could do this, you could do anything! What better power could you ask for? More importantly, if you recall, I told you to be yourself. Who are you? What are you? Anything you want to be. I hate to use somebody else's line, but-JUST DO IT! Here is something else for your consideration.

What do you think is the hardest type of speech to deliver? It is the speech you have to read! Can you imagine trying to keep eye contact with all those people while trying to stay word for word with a printed form? How can you do that? It is very difficult for even a seasoned veteran, so the answer is, do not try it! It will appear to your audience that you really know your subject, when you give them the impression you really do. It stands to reason, therefore, that if you have spent the time and studied your speech there is no reason to have to read it. You have learned it and know it! You have eliminated trying to look at two totally different things at the same time, and you have made yourself more confident about performing this presentation simply by knowing what it is you will talk about. Easy, isn't it? What could make more sense?

Why are you there? Has your boss commanded you to speak? Has someone discovered that you are a person with considerable knowledge about whatever it is that particular group needs to know about? Regardless of the reason, you are there for a purpose, and that purpose is to convey information, whether it is next year's budget, or some ball scores, to certain people. You owe it to those people to give them the information they require, and to give it to them in a form they can use. The audiences' obligation to you is to listen, and, if you perform your job well, their job will be made that much more easier. Is it not wonderful when both those obligations conclude at the same time?

If I tell you again, to practice and to be prepared, will you just think that I am being repetitious? Yes? Good! That is how important these elements are to you in order to learn the art of speaking in public. Do you sing in the shower? I do not want to get personal, but would that not be a wonderful time and place to practice a speech? PREPARE to the fullest extent of the word. You must know about the room in which you will speak, the people to whom you will be speaking, and why you will be speaking to them. Know the size of the room; where you will be waiting before you even get up to speak. Will you be sitting at a table within the group or will you already be up on the stage or near the speaker's position? If you are invited to eat before you are to speak, will you be affected in any way? How far away will you be from the audience during your talk, and will you have a microphone? What kind? If none, how loudly will you have to project your voice so the people in the very last row, however far, will be able to hear you comfortably? If at all possible, visit the room before your scheduled talk so these questions may be answered. To whom will you be speaking? How would you like to have been prepared to speak to a group of kids and wind up staring at a bunch of senior citizens? How happy would you be then? How happy would the senior citizens be? Always know who you will be speaking to, and how you will speak to them, relative to their level of understanding your subject. Make sure that you use language that they will understand, that is, avoid using too much, if any, slang to a group that you guess would not be familiar with those expressions. And, be friendly to them, whoever they are. Smile! That does not mean you have to be a comedian. Not everyone is a natural born comic. You may not own the knack for knowing just when to drop that funny line. In other words, not everyone can tell a joke. However, a talk can always be improved by adding a humorous story or a joke. As mentioned earlier, whenever you feel a need (during the planning of your talk) to do this, try to remember an event or situation that happened to you. A true event is always easier to relate than something you have to make up. All you need to do after you have chosen the story is to place it in the correct part of your speech. voila! You are a story teller! Once you get really good at this, you will be able to insert a funny story in the middle of a talk while you are actually talking to a group, because you will sense it is time for a laugh. Earlier I told a story about being lost when I was a kid growing up in Philadelphia. Not only is this a cute story, (I think so, anyway) it offers a moral which causes a smile. This story can be told in almost any situation, especially in a longer speech, simply by stopping at an appropriate time, looking out at the audience and asking, "By the way, folks, have I ever told you about the time I got lost?" This immediately puts the crowd on alert. Have I told them the story? They think for a second. They are paying even more attention to me now. No, they do not remember it. Now I am into the story and it ends eventually with the smile.

"Now, where was I? Oh yes, I was discussing .... So now the audience has had a little break, a little smile, they have heard something they do not have to remember. They have all been given a chance to catch their breaths, and, in an instant, I am back into the main body of my talk. You do not have to be a story teller like Jay Leno; you only have to be like the story teller you have always been! You must go over and over your talk every chance you have, and then do it again. When you have mastered the subject, you will find that these annoying, unnecessary sounds will disappear from your vocabulary. That will certainly be a plus! Just in case you have not realized it, all of the elements you are combining to make you a better speaker will also enable you to speak better, and with more confidence, in all walks of your life. Imagine, you have conquered the world's greatest fear! All by yourself! How motivating can that be? If you can accomplish beating the very thing that makes grown men and women cringe, throw up, get hives, etc, you can do anything! Once you set your mind to achieving that goal, there is no telling how far you can go. This is why I strongly urge youngsters, especially those in middle school, to start thinking about talking in front of groups. Imagine if the kids of today could eliminate the major fear of public communication, what a better world this will be!

Back in my younger days in Philadelphia, I once worked in a bakery and managed the plant which had many employees. One of them, a likable fellow named John, had a difficult time speaking to anyone because he was very shy. Every time he spoke, John prefaced each sentence with the words, "let's see"! "Good morning, John, how are you this fine day?" "Ah, let's see, I guess I'm doing all right." "Hey John, How 'bout them

Phillies last night?" "Let's see, yeh, they did OK!" I always think of John, especially during the time I spend listening to other speakers. Have you ever heard a nationally known speaker, on television, stutter through a speech with a bunch of ERs UHs or UMs? How difficult is it to listen and understand someone who obviously has not taken the time to put his/her thoughts together in a logical order so the listener can receive those thoughts properly. Remember I mentioned the subject of communication, which requires at least two people. One of the early steps was to create words from thoughts that could be comprehended fairly easily. If you are going to pass on a string of "well ah ... let me see ..... or the like, as well as what we refer to as audible pauses, er, ah, um; you will convince the audience that you have no idea about what it is you are trying to say.

OK, here is another reason to visit Toastmasters International! At each meeting, a previously appointed member keeps tabs on every speaker and counts the number of audible pauses, reporting that list at the end of the meeting. Each toastmaster must pay to the club five cents per AH! This is not an astounding amount of money, but it does make you think about it. Virtually every member, after awhile, can deliver a complete speech without those bothersome interruptions.

Consider the use of visual aids during the presentation of your talk. There is only one basic rule here and that is: Never show them what they can not see! What does that mean? It means never showing the photographs you shot while visiting the Rockies. Although it would be extremely difficult to show ANYTHING in print, I will tell you another story to illustrate the proper way to show your souvenirs to the audience. We're off!

"How many of you have ever had a city renamed in your honor? I have. Many years ago I lived in an apartment complex in New Jersey called "Cherrywood". For over three years I was the unofficial social director for that community, and we, my neighbors and I, partied quite frequently. I am sure you have seen those signs posted along a highway which announces that model apartments are open for your inspection, the direction to which is usually noted by a rather large arrow pointing to its location. Unbeknownst to me, certain residents of our community painted a garish gold color over many of those signs over which, in a darker color, they proclaimed that "JERRYWOOD" apartment models would be open today. I was honored by that event, along with the party that ensued. In fact, I still have a sign, actually taken from the White Horse Pike, and here it is!" The sign, by the way, had been tucked away behind the podium, OUT OF SIGHT, so that while I was speaking, people in the audience were not craning their necks trying to see just what that big yellow thing was. Once I have announce the fact that the item will now be shown, I lift it high so everyone in the room has a good look at it.

After I've waved it from left to right and back again, I return it, completely out of sight. I now have the full attention of my audience again. Back into the speech: "But that is not the award I wanted to tell you about tonight! Now I know that some of you have received commendations from your municipality, and so have I. Because I spent a few years coaching flag football for a group of ten to twelve year olds, I received this plaque from the city which sponsored the league. I will show it to you now." At this point, I reach behind me, pick up the plaque from where it has been kept OUT OF SIGHT, and hold it over my head so everyone can get a glimpse of it. (It's a brown framed citation written in green ink. (Really! Green ink!)) I move it from left to right and back again so the entire audience gets at least an idea about what it is I am trying to convey, and then I put it back down behind me OUT OF SIGHT, so it will not be a distraction and take away their attention. Has the point been made? Continuing: "But that is not the award I wanted to tell you about either." I now have a thread running through the speech which, while keeping the audience more in tune, waiting for the next 'but that is not the award....., but also provides a bit of humor. "Have any of you ever received the keys to a city? I have. You've seen those fake keys on TV shows, I'm sure. Well, because of some civic duties I performed for another of those cities down here in South Florida, I was once presented with the key to a city, and I'll never forget the moment. I do have that very key here with me, and, of course, I will show it to you now." Now I carefully get the foot and a half long, brown wooden key, festooned with bright red ribbon, from where it had been hiding, OUT OF SIGHT of the audience, hold it up over my head, swinging from left to right and back again, so everyone could see it. Then, back it goes, OUT OF SIGHT, so that the attention is back to me.

I think you now know how to present a visual aid. Now to finish the story with a strong ending. "But that is not the award I wanted to tell you about, tonight."

"Remember I told you I had formed a parents' group that numbered approximately eleven thousand people? During that time I had also enrolled as a student at Temple University. That school was situated near a neighborhood which was not conducive to late night strolling. One evening I was running a little late and was forced to locate a parking spot some distance from the school, not a pleasant situation. Later, when class was finished, I found myself in this unfriendly neighborhood after dark. I kept a wary eye as I proceeded to my car. Across the street, coming towards me, was a gang of teenagers. They were all looking at me." "I only worried slightly, until they started to walk across the street, directly toward me. Now I started to worry a lot! I had seen a lot of movies, however, and I quickly backed up against a store window so none of them could get behind me. Wasn't I smart? They now surrounded me in a semi circle. I started to perspire. One of the boys stepped forward. He asked, "Is your name Jerry Gold?" My heart came out of my throat and settled back into place. After I responded in the affirmative, he said that they had recognized me from my many appearances on television, (news events and such) realized I was a friend to all students, and wanted to come over and THANK ME! I literally danced the rest of the way to my car. What a lesson I learned about judging people! But, THAT is the award I wanted to share with you tonight. One I cannot actually show you, because it is here, in my heart!

Corny? Maybe so, but true.

Did I make the point about showing visual aids to your audience? I hope so. What if you do have photographs you want to share with the group? Here is what you tell them. "Folks, I do have pictures of the event, and I will be glad to share them with you after the presentation (meeting, dinner, etc.). OK?

When you are in the middle of a speech, you may suffer a momentary lapse. This will rarely occur. Seriously! When it happens just stop, look around (always smile), take a sip of water, all the while thinking, "I know this. Where am I in the narrative? You regroup, and move right along, picking up exactly where you left off. Why? Because you have practiced! You KNOW what it is you are taking about! Also, be concise. If you drag it out too long, you will lose the crowd. Tell them, and get out of there! But make sure you tell them in a way that will keep their interest level high. While you are talking you may decide to show exhibits or pictures. Remember, show only things that everyone in the room can see. You may even decide to answer questions. It will be up to you, normally, whether you want to do this during or after your talk. It will depend on time requirements. In any case, know what you are doing BEFORE you do it. It has got to come out right. Here is a little quote I heard somewhere, a long time ago. My apologies to whoever put these words together. TELL ME, I'LL LISTEN, SHOW ME, I'LL PAY ATTENTION, INVOLVE ME, I'LL LEARN. Isn't it a wonderful thing that you can do all three?

Because I know, beyond a reasonable doubt, that your quest to become a polished, professional speaker is insatiable, here is

DIRECTORY OF ASSOCIATION MEETING PLANNERS AND CONFERENCE &

CONVENTION DIRECTORS
121 CHANLON ROAD NEW PROVIDENCE, N.J. 07974

* * *

DIRECTOR OF CONVENTIONS
633 THIRD AVENUE
NEW YORK, NEW YORK 10017
CONVENTIONSOUTH
BOX 2267 GULF SHORES, AL. 36547
AND LET'S NOT FORGET OUR FRIENDS UP NORTH:
DIRECTORY OF ASSOCIATIONS IN CANADA
MICROMEDIA, LTD
20 VICTORIA STREET
TORONTO, ONTARIO, CANADA M5C 2NB

ALABAMA
2 N. Jackson, P.O. Box 76 Montgomery, 36101-0076
(334) 834-6000

ALASKA
217 2nd St. #201, Juneau, 99801
(907) 586-2323

AMERICAN SAMOA
P O Box 2446, Pago Pago, 96799
(684) 633 5583

ARIZONA
1221 E. Osborn Rd. #IOO, Phoenix, 85014
(602) 248-9172

ARKANSAS
410 S. Cross, PO Box 3645, Little Rock, 72203-3645
(501) 374-9225

CALIFORNIA
1201 K St.12th Fl. P.O. Box 1736, Sacramento, 95812
(916) 444-6670

COLORADO
1776 Lincoln St. # 1200 Denver, 80203-1029
(303) 831-7411

CONNECTICUT
370 Asylum St. Hartford, 06103-2022
(860) 244-1900

DELAWARE
1201 N. Orange St. P.O. Box 671 Wilmington, 19899-0671
(302) 655-7221

DISTRICT OF COLUMBIA
1301 Pennsylvania Ave. N.W. #309
(202) 347-7201

FLORIDA
136 S. Bronough St. P.O. Box 11309 Tallahassee, 32302-3309
(904) 425-1200

GEORGA
233 Peachtree St. #200 Atlanta, 30303-1504
(404) 223-2264

GUAM
Aspinall Ave. # 102, P.O. 283 Agama, 96910
(011) 671 472 6311

HAWAII
1132 Bishop St. #200 Honolulu, 96813-2830
(808) 545-4300

IDAHO
(No State chamber)

ILLINOIS
311 S. Wacker Dr. #1500, Chicago, 60606-6619
(312) 983 7100

INDIANA
One N. Capitol Ave. #200
Indianapolis, 46204-2248
(317) 264-3110

IOWA
200 E. Grand
Des Moines, 50309,
(515) 242 4700

KANSAS
835 S.W. Topeka Blvd
Topeka, 66612-1671
(913) 357-6321

KENTUCKY
464 Chenault Rd, PO Box 817
FRANKFORT, 40602-0817
(502) 695-4700

LOUISIANA
3113 Valley Creek Dr. P.O. 80258
Baton Rouge, 70898-0258,
(504) 928-5388

MAINE
7 Community Dr.
Augusta, 04330
(207) 623-4568

MARYLAND
60 West St. #100
Annapolis, 21401-2458
(410) 269-0642
MASSACHUSETTS
(No State Chamber)

MICHIGAN
600 S. Walnut St.
Lansing, 48933-2200
(517) 371-2100

MINNESOTA
30 E. 7th St. #1700
Saint Paul 55101
(800) 821-2230

MISSISSIPPI
P.O. Box 23276
Jackson, 39225-3276
(601) 969-0022

MISSOURI
428 E. Capitol Ave. P.O. Box 149
Jefferson City, 65102
(573) 634-3511

MONTANA
2030 11th Ave., P.O. Box 1730
Helena, 59601
(406) 442-2405

NEBRASKA
P.O. Box 95128
Lincoln, 68509
(402) 474-4422

NEVADA
P.O. Box 3499
Reno, 89505
(702) 686-3030

NEW HAMPSHIRE
122 N. Main
Concord, 03301
(603) 224-5388

NEW JERSEY
50 W. State St. # 1310
Trenton, 08608-1214
(609) 989-7888

NEW MEXICO
2309 Rennard Pl. SE #402
Albuquerque, 87106-4259
(505) 842-0644

NEW YORK
(No State Chamber)

NORTH CAROLINA
225 Hillsborough St. P.O. Box 2508
Raleigh, 27602-2508
(919) 836-1425

NORTH DAKOTA
2000 Schafer St. P.O. Box 2639
Bismarck, 58502
(701) 222-0929

OHIO
P.O. Box 15159
Columbus, 43215-0159
(614) 228-4201

OKLAHOMA
330 NE 10th St.
Oklahoma City, 73104-3200
(405) 235-3669

OREGON
(No State Chamber)

PENNSYLVANIA
417 Walnut St.
Harrisburg, 17101-1902
(800) 225-7224

SOUTH CAROLINA
1201 Main St. #1810
Columbia, 29201-3254
(803) 799-4601

SOUTH DAKOTA
P.O. Box 190
Pierre, 57501-0190
(800) 742-81120

TENNESSEE
(No State Chamber)

TEXAS
400 W. 15th #910
Austin, 78701-1647
(512) 477-6721

UTAH
P.O. Box 310
West Jordan, 84084-0310
(801) 569-5151

VERMONT
P.O. Box 37
Montpelier, 05601
(802) 223-3443

VIRGIN ISLANDS
6-7 Dronningens Gate P.O. Box 324
St. Thomas, 00804-0324
(809) 776-0100

VIRGIN ISLANDS
Kings Hill, P.O. Box 4369
St. Croix, 00851-4369
(809) 773-1435

VIRGINIA
9 S. 5th St.
Richmond, 23219
(804) 644-1607

WASHINGTON
1414 S. Cherry St. P.O. Box 658
Olympia, 98507-0658
(360) 943-1600

WEST VIRGINIA
P.O. Box 2789
Charleston, 25330
(304) 342-1115

You should always keep in touch with the local Chambers of Commerce. They will know, and will be thrilled to share with you, times and dates of all area groups which may be searching for a speaker. Major businesses are also receptive to presentations that will motivate or invigorate their staff, especially one that is geared to raise production. Create a nice looking brochure and send a copy to anyone you can think of who may conduct regularly scheduled meetings.

Do not forget other clubs in the area that almost always look for speakers, for example:

ELKS CLUBS

KIWANIS CLUBS

ROTARY

YOUR TOWN'S JAYCEES

AMERICAN LEGION

FRIENDS OF YOUR LOCAL LIBRARY

ANY LOCAL LADIES CLUBS

Contact them and assure them you can ***TELL 'EM ABOUT IT!***

www.ingramcontent.com/pod-product-compliance
Lightning Source LLC
Chambersburg PA
CBHW031241280526
45784CB00004B/1671

* 9 7 8 0 5 9 5 1 8 2 7 5 6 *